My Feelings

CW00863520

WHEN I FEEL HAPPY

Amy Beattie

E **Enslow Publishing**
101 W. 23rd Street
Suite 240
New York, NY 10011
USA

enslow.com

Published in 2020 by Enslow Publishing, LLC
101 W. 23rd Street, Suite 240, New York, NY 10011

Library of Congress Cataloging-in-Publication Data

Names: Beattie, Amy, author.
Title: When I feel happy / Amy Beattie.
Description: New York : Enslow Publishing, 2020. | Series: My feelings |
Includes bibliographical references and index. | Audience: Grades K–2.
Identifiers: LCCN 2019007731| ISBN 9781978511583 (library bound) | ISBN
9781978511552 (pbk.) | ISBN 9781978511569 (6 pack)
Subjects: LCSH: Happiness in children—Juvenile literature. |
Happiness—Juvenile literature.
Classification: LCC BF723.H37 B43 2020 | DDC 155.4/19—dc23
LC record available at https://lccn.loc.gov/2019007731

Printed in the United States of America

To Our Readers: We have done our best to make sure all websites in this book were active and appropriate when we went to press. However, the author and the publisher have no control over and assume no liability for the material available on those websites or on any websites they may link to. Any comments or suggestions can be sent by email to customerservice@enslow.com.

Photo Credits: Cover wavebreakmedia/Shutterstock.com; pp. 4, 5 Yuganov Konstantin/Shutterstock.com; pp. 6, 9 Syda Productions/Shutterstock.com; pp. 7, 8 JF Jacobsz/Shutterstock.com; pp. 10, 11 Littlekidmoment/Shutterstock.com; pp. 12, 13, 14, 15 Milatas/Getty Images; p. 16 Ginny Filer/Shutterstock.com; p. 17 LightField Studios/Shutterstock.com; p. 18 Rido/Shutterstock.com; p. 19 pim pic/Shutterstock.com; p. 20 ZouZou/Shutterstock.com; p. 21 Monkey Business Images/Shutterstock.com; pp. 22, 23 Sunny studio/Shutterstock.com; cover, p. 1 (emoji) Cosmic_Design/Shutterstock.com.

Contents

Snow Day 4

Our Family Dog 6

Making a Present 10

Playing Baseball 12

Baby Cousin 16

Learning to Write 18

Learning Math 20

Being Happy 22

Words to Know 24

Index 24

I feel happy when it snows. It looks so pretty outside.

We get a snow day from school. I go sledding with my friends. Even though it is cold, we have fun playing together.

I feel happy when my family gets a dog. We name her Molly.

My daddy says she gets scared when I shout.
She is shy around new people.

Daddy says I should wait for her to come to me. Maybe she will play **fetch**. I throw a ball for her. She goes to get it.

I know she will be happy living with us. We are going to be such good friends!

I feel happy when I make a present for my brother.

He is so excited when he opens it! Next time we will make **origami** together.

I feel happy when my friends and I play baseball together.

Baseball is my favorite game. Even if I drop the ball, I still have fun.

My friend Jack is not very good at catching the ball. We play together and practice.

Jack's favorite game is soccer. We will play soccer tomorrow. Everyone gets a chance to choose what game to play. We can all learn new games together.

I feel happy when my cousin has a baby. I can hold the baby if I am very careful.

When the baby grows up, we will play games together. Maybe the baby will play with my brother and sister.

I feel happy when I learn to write letters.

Now I want to learn to write out words! My dad helps me spell out "DAD." I cannot wait until I know enough words to write my own story.

I feel happy when I learn how to add numbers.

My teacher helps all of us work with numbers.
I am happy when I get better at math.

Many flowers make me feel happy.

I feel happy in water. I feel happy when other people feel happy, too.

Words to Know

fetch A ball game to play with a dog.

origami Folding paper into shapes.

Index

baby, 16–17
baseball, 12–14
dog, 6–9
family, 6
flowers, 22

friends, 5, 12, 14
numbers, 20–21
playing, 5, 8, 12, 14, 15, 17
snow, 4–5

soccer, 15
water, 23
writing, 18–19

Chapter 1

"Ouch, that hurt!". Amadeus pulled his tentacles into his chest and rested for a moment.

He had been practising swimming in the swirling sea current, and it was proving to be much more difficult than he had thought. His mum had said he should swim by puffing water out of his mouth, but Amadeus still found it easier to try and swim with his tentacles.

However, the problem with being a Jurassic ammonite was that whichever way you swam, you always swam backwards, and Amadeus didn't really think this was very sensible.

"I know it means my shell hits the rocks first instead of my head, but I can't see where I am going and it makes my bottom slam into the inside of my shell" he said to himself as he wriggled in his shell to ease the pain.

As he wriggled he noticed that Beate was laughing at him. Beate always laughed at him. As usual he blushed and went red.

3

He liked Beate, they lived next door to each other and often played together in the shelter of the large rocks.

"Why are you always watching when I do something wrong?" he called across to her.

"Why do you always do something silly when I'm watching" she called back laughing.

Amadeus turned around, embarrassed, and started swimming back to the shelter of the rocks where he lived with his mum and dad. The rocks were in part of the sea called 'The Ven', and were surrounded by miles of soft muddy sea bed.

Many different sea creatures lived at The Ven. There were several families of ammonites, and also lots of belemnites like Beate and her family. The belemnites tended to think they were better than ammonites as their sleek bodies meant they could swim faster. However, ammonites had their tricks too, as Amadeus could use a little puff of his tummy wind to fill his shell with gas and make himself float. If he squished the gas with some water he could sink back down.

When Amadeus was smaller he remembered his uncle Gregor used to eat big mouthfuls of Spungroot seaweed. After a little while it would give him really bad tummy wind, and he would roar with laughter as he filled his shell and went shooting up to the surface of the sea.

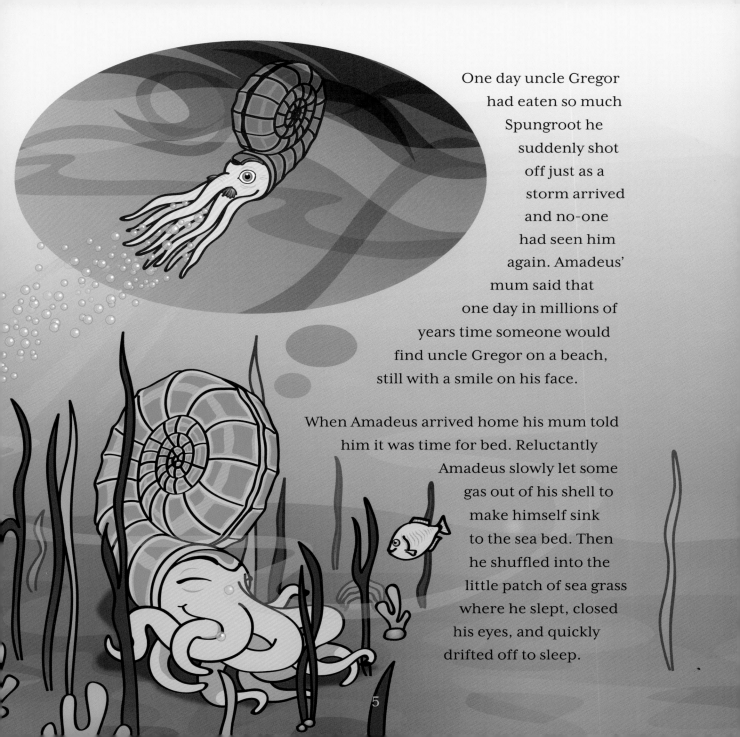

One day uncle Gregor had eaten so much Spungroot he suddenly shot off just as a storm arrived and no-one had seen him again. Amadeus' mum said that one day in millions of years time someone would find uncle Gregor on a beach, still with a smile on his face.

When Amadeus arrived home his mum told him it was time for bed. Reluctantly Amadeus slowly let some gas out of his shell to make himself sink to the sea bed. Then he shuffled into the little patch of sea grass where he slept, closed his eyes, and quickly drifted off to sleep.

Chapter 2

The big sea dragon pulled his mouth into a nasty grin. Big sharp teeth filled his mouth. His large eyes made him look really mean. Suddenly he dived forward straight towards Amadeus, the water was swirling, big teeth were flashing centimetres from his face, pieces of shell and stone from the sea bed were hammering against Amadeus' shell. "No don't eat me, I haven't even learnt to swim properly" Amadeus shouted at the sea dragon.

Suddenly Amadeus slammed into something hard which sent pain right through his body. He opened his eyes expecting to see the inside of the sea dragon's mouth. But instead he saw The Ven in chaos. The sea dragon had been a dream, but this seemed even worse. The sea bed must have heaved, as it sometimes did causing big valleys to open up, but this must have been a big one.

Seaweed, stones, sand and mud flew around in a violent rage. Brachiken, a 'shell-hermit' who usually lived attached to a rock nearby, flew past caught in an invisible current. A piece of rock broke off a big sea stack and crashed into the seabed causing even more mud to swirl up in an enormous black cloud.

"Help!" Amadeus shouted.
But everything was dark, the
mud had completely blocked out
the light from above, and Amadeus could
feel himself being washed along in a strong current.

Amadeus was scared. He was so scared his tummy let out a little
puff of tummy gas, and he felt himself starting to rise towards
the surface. Then another little puff and he was rising faster.
But the more he went up the more violent the sea became.

Slowly it started to get lighter, and much more frightening. The sea
was crashing backwards and forwards rather than in a smooth flow.
He could see enormous waves on the surface crashing down, filling
the water above him with bubbles as big as the sea dragon. "Never go to
the surface" his mum always said, but here he was hurtling upwards.

7

"I've got to do something.
Never go to the surface"
Amadeus shouted. "I've got
to let the gas out" he shouted
even louder. He wasn't sure
who he was shouting at, it just
seemed that if he shouted as loud
as he could it would help somehow.

Amadeus calmed himself and started to squeeze
gently so little bubbles appeared as his tummy gas
started to leak from his shell. Slowly he stopped rising
towards the surface, and he kept squeezing to push more gas out.

Eventually he started to sink again, but he was still caught in a strong
current, and he could do nothing except let the current carry him
through the sea. After floating for a while surrounded by debris
and bits of seaweed he had sunk enough to reach the sea bed.

Amadeus started to bump along in the mud. Each time he
hit the bottom a black cloud would appear and he would
bounce back up a few centimetres. Then he would sink and
bump into the mud again producing another cloud.

"Oh I just wish I could stop" thought Amadeus
as he continued to bounce along.

BANG! OUCH! Amadeus had hit something hard, and once again his bottom continued moving after his shell stopped. "Oh my bottom!" he said. "I wish that didn't keep happening". He started wriggling and easing his bottom back to where it should be in the shell.

Once comfortable he looked around. He had come to rest at the bottom of a large outcrop of rock. The current was holding him against the rock as mud and bits of seabed flew past, so he decided to stay still and rub his aches and pains.

Chapter 3

Amadeus had drifted into a deep sleep, but this time there were no sea dragons in his dreams. He dreamt he was drifting through a beautiful sea, full of bright colours. Brightly coloured fish swam in brightly coloured sea grass. Colourful rays shone down from above onto sparkling coral.

Amadeus awoke, yawned and stretched his tentacles. The sea storm had subsided and everything was calm, so he felt much more relaxed. He looked about him, but he didn't recognise anything. There was no mud here, just tiny stones, which made the sea bed smooth, with just a few small ripples caused by the currents.

"Oh where am I?" thought Amadeus, a little bit of fear creeping into his voice. "Oh no" he thought, "I must not get scared or I'll start floating".

He sat for a while wondering if his mum and dad would come and get him. "Perhaps they will be here soon" he thought. But inside he had a strange feeling that he was now all alone. Alone in a big sea, hardly able to swim, and in a strange place.

"What creatures live here?" "Are they friendly?"
"Will they eat me?" "Is this where the sea dragon lives?"

Amadeus sat and thought. He thought about what he should think about. He thought that he should probably think of an idea. So he thought about how he should think of an idea. Then he thought about what idea he should think of if he thought of an idea.

Clearly this was getting him nowhere. But it did calm his tummy gas so he stayed on the seabed. "Perhaps I should have a little swim and explore this strange place" he thought. "After all, other than this rock, there is not much to bump in to. I'll go in a minute after I've had a rest".

11

After five minutes he thought "I'll go in another
minute, I'll have more energy".

After another five minutes he thought "maybe the current
has picked up, I'll give it another minute or two".

Nearly an hour later Amadeus slowly started to swim. Backwards.
Ammonites always swam backwards. Tentacles in, tentacles out,
little puff of water. Tentacles in, tentacles out, little puff of water.
Gradually he picked up speed and started to look around.

The sea was big, empty, and clear.
Well it was where he had just
come from, as he could only
look backwards. Tentacles
in, tentacles out, puff.

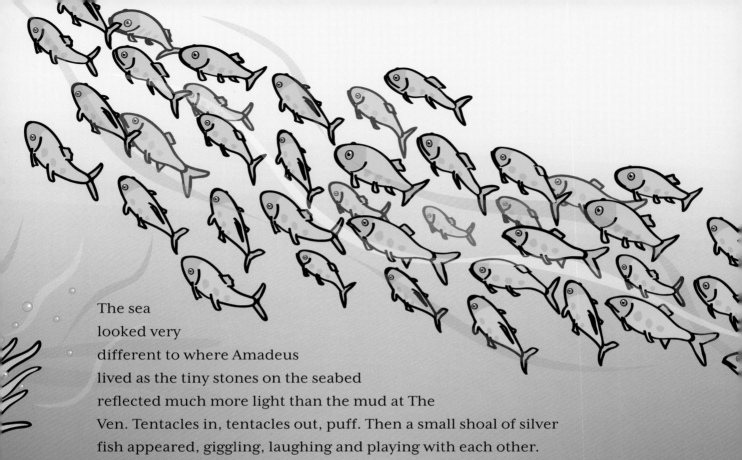

The sea
looked very
different to where Amadeus
lived as the tiny stones on the seabed
reflected much more light than the mud at The
Ven. Tentacles in, tentacles out, puff. Then a small shoal of silver
fish appeared, giggling, laughing and playing with each other.

"Hey, where am I" Amadeus called out. The fish ignored him and
disappeared into the distance. Amadeus carried on swimming,
tentacles in, tentacles out, puff. Tentacles in, tentacles out, puff.

From the corner of his eye he saw a large fish approaching. This fish was
at least ten times as big as Amadeus, and his size frightened Amadeus
so he pulled his head and tentacles back into his shell. Amadeus
thought that if he couldn't see the fish, the fish might not see him.

"What are you doing here little one?". It was the fish.
Was he speaking to Amadeus or someone else?
Amadeus stayed hidden in his shell and didn't answer.

All of a sudden there was a 'Thwack' on his shell as the fish flicked
it with his tail. "You in there. I'm speaking to you, stop hiding
like a baby". That annoyed Amadeus. How dare the fish call him
a baby, he'd show him, he'd show the fish how angry he could be,
he'd show him what happened if you called him a baby, he'd....

But he didn't. He stayed in his shell and didn't make a sound. "Oh
well it's up to you if you don't want to talk" said the fish, and Amadeus
felt a swirl around him as the fish flicked its tail and swam away.

All alone again Amadeus slowly stretched his head and tentacles out of his shell and looked around. Clear sea and little stones. "Oh how am I going to get home again" Amadeus thought.

Chapter 4

As Amadeus looked around he saw a field of sea grass nearby. Sand fleas hid in sea grass, and as he was hungry Amadeus swam over.

When he got there, he found it was unlike any sea grass or seaweed he had seen before. There were long stems with plumes like ferns forming heads at the top. These must be the Sea Lilies that he had heard his mum talk about.

Amadeus swam into the middle of the Sea Lilies, and hid, ready to pounce with his tentacles if a sand flea came near. He stayed very still, while the Sea Lilies fluttered in the gentle current.

As he hid Amadeus had a strange feeling that the Sea Lilies were stroking and feeling the back of his shell. He thought it must just be the current making them rub against him as he stayed so still.

Suddenly Amadeus saw something move. It was a sand flea, and it was hopping between the stems of the Sea Lilies. Amadeus held his breath, and waited.

The sand flea jumped nearer. "One more jump and I'll have you" thought Amadeus. It jumped up, about to fly over the top of a Sea Lily straight into Amadeus' waiting tentacles. But as it jumped the Sea Lily suddenly moved and somehow the sand flea disappeared.

"Well that's weird" thought Amadeus. "What made the Sea Lily suddenly sway like that, and where has the sand flea gone?"

He settled down again and waited for another sand flea. Sure enough after a few minutes another one appeared. It too hopped towards Amadeus' waiting tentacles. Then at the last minute, just as it jumped, the Sea Lily reached out, grabbed the sand flea and popped it into a large mouth that opened in the centre of its plumes.

"Oh no, it's not a plant, it's an animal that eats other creatures!"
shouted Amadeus, but as he tried to move he felt tentacles
from other Sea Lilies wrapping themselves around his shell.

He struggled with his own tentacles, trying to break
free, but the Sea Lilies started to pull him backwards,
holding him tighter and tighter. "Help!" he
shouted as he suddenly got very frightened.
Images flashed through his mind
of being eaten by the creatures
that looked like plants.

18

Amadeus got so frightened that he puffed
a little tummy wind into his shell. That
combined with his thrashing tentacles
suddenly made him break free from the
grabbing Sea Lilies and he shot upwards.

As soon as he got control of himself he swam away
from the field of Sea Lilies as fast as he could,
only resting again once he was in the open sea.

"That was close" he thought to himself,
"I was almost eaten alive".

19

Chapter 5

Amadeus started swimming again. Tentacles in, tentacles out, puff. Tentacles in, tentacles out, puff.

In the distance he saw the sea was cloudy as though something was disturbing the bottom causing bits of old seaweed and debris to swirl in the water.

Tentacles in, tentacles out, puff. Tentacles in, tentacles out, puff. He should be getting further away as he was facing backwards and swimming away from it, but the cloud seemed to be getting nearer. Surely it couldn't?

Tentacles in, tentacles out, puff. Tentacles in, tentacles out, puff. No, it was definitely getting closer, Amadeus felt a bit scared and as a result floated up a little bit.

The cloud was getting
closer and closer.
Were those eyes he
could see in the cloud?
Did he see the jagged
outline of sharp teeth?

"Swim, swim, swim"
he thought, pushing his
tentacles in and out as fast as
he could, and puffing water from
his mouth to get more speed.

The cloud continued to grow. Bigger and bigger
it got, closer and closer. Amadeus closed his eyes to force
all his strength into swimming and puffing little squirts of water with his
mouth. Tentacles in, tentacles out, puff. Tentacles in, tentacles out, puff.

As he swam he felt the water pushing him faster. But
what was pushing the water behind him?

Amadeus opened his eyes and screamed. An enormous mouth, long sharp teeth, evil eyes. It was the sea dragon and it was about to eat him!

He didn't have time to do anything. The mouth was open wide and Amadeus was swept in, straight past the sharp teeth and into the sea dragon's tummy.

It was very dark in the sea dragon's tummy and Amadeus was frightened.

Chapter 6

"Not even worth chewing"
the sea dragon thought to
himself. "Silly little ammonite
thought he could out-swim a Sea
Dragon. That will teach him".

"I think I'll go and see where
yesterday's sea tremor happened. There
is usually a big crack in the sea floor to
investigate when sea tremors happen".

So off the sea dragon swam. His big powerful
body eased him along faster than any of the
other creatures in the sea. Most of the other creatures
disappeared beneath rocks or into seaweed when they saw
him coming, but if they didn't, he gave them an enormous,
but not very friendly, grin with his mouth pulled back over
his long pointed teeth. They soon moved out of the way then.

The sea dragon knew these waters well, as he often made the
long journey from the Folk Stone in the east to the great
wall of Sea Corn in the west. He swam for hours, with
the bright sun illuminating the water in front of him.
Later that afternoon it gradually started to get dark.

The shadows that the rocks made on the sea bed got longer and longer, and even though the sea dragon had enormous eyes above his enormous teeth, it became harder and harder to see where he was going.

Finally he reached a place where he had rested before. It was a quiet sheltered spot where he knew he could get a good night's sleep, and so he stopped swimming, stretched his flippers, and settled down to doze.

"Hmmm, a nice tasty mouthful of belemnites, followed by the head of a large ammonite" he dreamed to himself. He liked dreaming about food it made him sleep better, and he always felt better in the morning when he awoke.

"Big tasty ammonite......
ZzzzzZZZZZZzz" He started snoring. "Gnoooocccchh zzzzzZZZZZZ".
"Gnoooocccchh zzzzzZZZZZZ".

Amadeus had been dozing himself inside the tummy of the sea dragon. It had been quite

24

relaxing in the dark, except when the sea dragon opened his mouth to show his teeth to other creatures. Then the sea came rushing in, and washed Amadeus around the sea dragon's tummy.

But now the sea dragon seemed to be asleep and snoring. His mouth opened, "**Gnoooocccchh**", and the sea came rushing in. Then "**zzzzzZZZZZZ**" as the sea rushed out again and the mouth shut.

Amadeus waited and watched.

"**Gnooooccccchh**" sea in, "**zzzzzZZZZZZ**" sea out. "**Gnooooccccchh**" sea in, "**zzzzzZZZZZZ**" sea out. "**Gnooooccccchh**" sea in, "**zzzzzZZZZZZ**" sea out.

"This is my chance" thought Amadeus. He held on to the side of the sea dragon's tummy "**Gnooooccccchh**" the sea came rushing in, then he let go "**zzzzzZZZZZZ**" and it rushed out. Yes! He was washed nearer to the mouth!

He held on again, "**Gnooooccccchh**" then he let go "**zzzzzZZZZZZ**" and again was washed towards the mouth. He did this another three times until he was inside the sea dragon's big mouth, with the long sharp teeth all around him.

"One more and I'll be out" he thought. He held on tight "**Gnooooccccchh**". Then he let go "**zzzZZ**".

"Oh no, it's only breathed out a little, I'm not going to get past the teeth!". Sure enough the mouth closed and the teeth came crashing down on

25

Amadeus who just closed his eyes as there was nothing else he could do.

"Am I dead?" he thought. "I didn't feel much when he bit me in half". He opened one eye. He saw an enormous tooth. He closed that eye and opened his other eye. He saw another enormous tooth. "Oh I must be dead" he thought. "I'll never see mum and dad again". He started to feel very sad.

Then he opened both eyes and looked again. He realised that he was stuck in the gap between the two teeth. He wasn't dead! He didn't even have a tooth through his tummy! But he was very stuck.

"I'll swim free" he thought. Tentacles in, tentacles out, puff. Tentacles in, tentacles out, puff. He looked again. He hadn't moved. Tentacles in, tentacles out, puff. Tentacles in, tentacles out, puff. Once again he opened his eyes and looked. Nothing.

He sat back and rested. "What can I do?" he wondered. "I'm going to be stuck in the sea dragon's mouth for the rest of my life, which won't be very long if the top teeth come down on me".

Then he heard a strange deep rumble. **Brrrruuughhhh**. "What's that?" he thought. It seemed to come from deeper in the sea dragon's tummy. **Brrrruuughhhh**. There it was again. Then suddenly **BUUUURRRRRRPPPPPP** the sea dragon did an enormous burp. Water and bits of the sea dragon's dinner came rushing up, bashed into Amadeus and washed him clean out of the sea dragon's mouth.

He was free! But he was also right in front of
the sea dragon's teeth. He felt scared. "Oh no, I'm not
doing that" he thought as a bit of tummy wind started to
form. He squeezed hard, blew a bit of gas
out of his shell, and swam as fast
as he could to some weed he
could see on the sea bed.

Chapter 7

Amadeus hid for hours. "**Gnooooccccchh zzzzzZZZZZ**" came the noise from above him. "Surely nothing can sleep with that noise" he thought, as he hid in the seaweed, trying desperately not to get too scared. But he was so exhausted that eventually he too dozed off. It wasn't a good sleep, but it was sleep and at least he couldn't hear the "**Gnooooccccchh zzzzzZZZZZ**".

When he awoke the sun was up and the sea was bright. Carefully Amadeus looked out from the seaweed. The sea dragon had gone! "Oh I'm saved" shouted Amadeus.

"Saved from what?" – it was Beate. What was she doing here? Had she been eaten by a sea dragon and burped back out as well?

"Your mum is going to kill you" she said. "You stayed out all of yesterday and didn't tell anyone where you were going, even though there was a sea storm! And here you are hiding on the other side of The Ven".

She turned her back (or was it her front?) and swam away.

Amadeus realised that he knew where he was, so he slowly swam out of the weed and across The Ven back towards home. "There you are!" his mum shouted. "Come here you naughty boy, you know I've told you never to go out in a sea storm, you could get washed away".

"But I was mum, I was washed away, miles and miles away, and I didn't know where I was, and I had to swim on my own, and the fish wouldn't talk to me, and a sea dragon came along and ate me, and I nearly escaped when he was snoring, but I got stuck in his teeth, and then he burped me out!".

His mum looked at him, unsure whether to laugh at his ridiculous story, or punish him for staying out on his own. Eventually she decided having him safe was what she really wanted and she had better things to do than continue to moan at him, so she went back to tidying their home after the sea storm.

Later that day Amadeus was sulking by the rocks when his dad came home. His dad put his tentacles around him, gave him a hug and said "Been dreaming again have you? Serves you right for going out in a storm and falling asleep". He laughed and swam away.

As his dad disappeared into their home in the seaweed Amadeus called out "It wasn't a dream".

But was it...?